# Squeeze Out

# Squeeze Out

80 juices to extract the best for your life

Susannah Blake

MQP

Published by **MQ Publications Limited**
12 The Ivories, 6–8 Northampton Street
London N1 2HY
Tel: 44 (0)20 7359 2244
Fax: 44 (0)20 7359 1616
email: mail@mqpublications.com
website: www.mqpublications.com

Copyright © MQ Publications Limited 2005
Text copyright © Susannah Blake 2005

Design and illustration: Jo Hill
Photography: Janine Hosegood
Home Economy: Jenny White

ISBN: 1-84072-793-4

1 3 5 7 9 0 8 6 4 2

Printed and bound in France by *Partenaires-Livres*® (JL)

This book contains the opinions and ideas of the author. It is intended to
provide helpful and informative material on the subjects addressed in
this book and is sold with the understanding that the author and
publisher are not engaged in rendering any kind of personal
professional services in this book. The author and publisher disclaim all
responsibility for any liability, loss, or risk, personal or otherwise, which
is incurred as a consequence, directly or indirectly, of the use and
application of any of the contents of this book.

# Introduction

There's nothing better than a tall glass of juice squeezed from fabulously fresh fruit and veg, or a thick and creamy, juicy smoothie made with blended fruits and mild, cool yogurt. Not only is the taste a little sip of heaven, but juices are unbelievably good for you, too! There's no wicked side to juice-drinking, it's just pure pleasure all the way.

Each juice in this book is blended with good health in mind, providing you with the perfect balance of nutrients to pick you up, calm you down, indulge your feel-good side, or cleanse your wicked side. Some of the detoxifiers might take a bit of getting used to—but your liver will love you for it! No matter what you're in the mood for, you're sure to find the perfect blend among these pages.

An electric juicer is easy to use and no trouble to clean—as long as you wash it up as soon as you've finished juicing! The other golden rule is "wash your veg." There's no point in making healing juices if they're full of fertilizer. Peel or scrub root vegetables and wash soft fruits and vegetables in soapy water—or, better still, buy organic. And last but not least, to reap the full benefits of a juice, be sure to drink it within 15 minutes of making it.

# 1

# **Daring Detox**

Cleansing tonics & purifying potions

# Wheatgrass Shooter

**A shot of this juice and your body won't know what's hit it. Renowned for its detoxifying properties, wheatgrass is the king of cleansers. It's powerful stuff though, so sip this juice slowly as some people can feel slightly nauseous and light-headed the first time they try it. You need an awful lot of wheatgrass to make a small glass—but the benefits are worth the effort!**

MAKES 1 SHOT

2 cups/80g wheatgrass

**1** Push small handfuls of the wheatgrass through a juicer. (Juicing wheatgrass is a tough job so you'll need a powerful juicer. Don't try to juice too much grass at once, as it can get caught up in some machines.) Pour into a shot glass and drink straight away, taking tiny sips.

## Growing your own wheatgrass

You can often buy trays of wheatgrass from health-food and organic stores, but it is easy to grow your own at home. Place 9oz/250g whole wheat grains in a bowl, pour over cold water and leave to soak for 24 hours. Fill a tray (measuring about 12 × 16in/30 × 40cm) with about 1½ in/4cm organic compost and spray lightly with water. Drain the wheat grains and scatter them over the compost, pressing them in slightly. Leave in a warm, sunny place. Check every day and spray with water. (Be careful not to overwater.) In less than a week, you should have a tray full of wheatgrass ready for juicing.

Wheatgrass Shooter

Lazy Liver Livener

# Lazy Liver Livener

Every ingredient in this cleansing juice helps to stimulate the liver and remove toxins from the body. Milk thistle, which is available from health-food stores, is an important liver-supporting herb. Tomatoes, carrots, and celery stimulate the liver, and apples help to remove toxins from it.

**MAKES 1 GLASS**

½ apple
2 carrots, trimmed
½ cup baby tomatoes
2 celery sticks
¼ tsp milk thistle extract
Celery stick, to serve

**1** Roughly chop the apple and carrots. Press the tomatoes through a juicer, followed by the apple, carrots, and celery.

**2** Stir the milk thistle extract into the juice, then pour into a glass and add a leafy celery stick as a healthy, liver-stimulating stirrer.

# Sprouts a-go-go

When it comes to juicing, wheatgrass sprouted from whole wheat grain is the real super-detoxifier—but for those who find its flavor just a little too intoxicating, try this milder version made with wheatgrass, alfalfa sprouts, and fennel. It's mild and refreshing and a fantastic detox juice in its own right.

**MAKES 1 GLASS**

¾ fennel bulb
¾ cup/30g wheatgrass
1½ cups/100g alfalfa

**1** Roughly chop the fennel bulb. Press the wheatgrass through a juicer, followed by the alfalfa, and then the fennel.

**2** Stir the juices to combine, then pour into a small glass and serve immediately.

# Green for Go

Adding spirulina to this vibrant green juice transforms it from a healthy cleanser into a turbo-charged power-purifier. Combining iron-rich spinach with vitamin C-rich apples helps to ensure the maximum absorption of nutrients, and also makes a deliciously mild, fruity blend.

**MAKES 1 TALL GLASS**

3 cups/120g baby spinach, plus
    extra to garnish (optional)
3 small dessert apples
¼ tsp spirulina

1 Wash the spinach and drain well, then roughly chop the apples. Press the spinach through a juicer, alternating with chunks of apple.

2 Stir the spirulina into the juice and pour into a tall glass. Garnish with a few baby spinach leaves, if liked, and serve.

# Strong Medicine

Not to everybody's taste, this strong, bitter, peppery juice can take a little getting used to. But the benefits really do outweigh the tingling effect it has on the taste buds. Celery cleanses and supports the liver, and helps flush out toxins at the same time. Watercress is packed with magnesium, calcium and iron, and also contains sulfur, which helps to rejuvenate the hair and nails.

**MAKES 1 GLASS**

⅓ cup/20g watercress
5 celery sticks
Ice cubes, to serve (optional)

1 Press the watercress through a juicer, followed by the celery sticks.

2 Pour into a glass and add a few ice cubes, if you like. Sip slowly, or gulp down as quickly as you can.

Green for Go

Vampire Juice

# Vampire Juice

You need only a small glass of this nutrient-rich, blood-red tonic to put your body to rights. Peppery, sweet, sharp, rich, and garlicky—sip it slowly to really appreciate the flavors. Beet is a great detoxifier and has long been used as a blood fortifier in traditional medicine, whereas celery is valued for its cleansing properties. Garlic has natural antibacterial and antifungal properties and adds a delicious bite.

**MAKES 1 SMALL GLASS**

½ orange
1 tomato
1 large beet
1 garlic clove, peeled
1 celery stick

1 Remove the peel from the orange and chop the tomato and beet into rough chunks.

2 Press the garlic through a juicer, followed by the orange, beet, tomato, and celery. Stir the juice, pour into a small glass and sip slowly.

# Ginger Geronimo

This fiery, ferocious blend isn't for the faint-hearted. Ginger is one of the detox super-spices, helping to cleanse the body and stimulate the digestive system. It's also a real warmer and can help to boost the circulation. Melons are a natural diuretic and help to flush out toxins from the liver.

**MAKES 1 GLASS**

¼–½in/5mm–1cm fresh root ginger
1 large slice rockmelon (about 6oz/200g)

1 Thinly peel the ginger. Scoop out the seeds from the melon, remove the rind and cut the flesh into large chunks.

2 Press the ginger through a juicer followed by the melon. Stir and pour into a small glass.

# Sugar Snap Flush

Fennel helps to flush toxins out of the system, while calming the stomach at the same time. Paired with sweet, stimulating sugar snap peas and kidney-boosting asparagus, it makes a deliciously refreshing, aniseed-flavored juice.

**MAKES 1 GLASS**

1 fennel bulb
1 cup/120g sugar snap peas
3 asparagus spears, plus
  1 spear to serve

**1** Roughly chop the fennel. Push the sugar snaps through the juicer, followed by the asparagus and chunks of fennel.

**2** Stir the juice, then pour into a glass and serve immediately with an extra asparagus spear to stir.

# Radish Revolution

More medicinal than refreshing, this peppery pink juice will do you the power of good. Artichokes have a natural cleansing effect and are said to help liver complaints—and hangovers! Sweet, peppery radishes are another liver-booster, whereas cabbage is a natural healer packed with health-giving nutrients.

**MAKES 1 SMALL GLASS**

½ cup/65g radishes
5½oz/150g white cabbage
1 globe artichoke

**1** Halve any large radishes and roughly chop the cabbage. Trim the base from the artichoke and peel away the leaves. Scoop out the hairy choke, and then cut the heart into quarters.

**2** Press the artichoke quarters through the juicer, followed by the radishes and cabbage. Stir, then pour into a glass and serve immediately.

Sugar Snap Flush

Spicy Carrot Clean

# Spicy Carrot Clean

Carrots, apples, and pears are packed with nutrients and have the added bonus of being great detoxifiers. Drink a large glass of this sweet, mild juice and feel its cleansing action start to work almost immediately. Pears are said to ensure a clear complexion and glossy hair too so you'll notice the benefits in no time.

**MAKES 1 TALL GLASS**

¾in/2cm piece fresh root
  ginger
3 large carrots
1 sharp-tasting dessert apple
1 pear
1 baby carrot with green
  leaves, to serve (optional)

**1** Thinly peel the ginger, then scrub the carrots well and remove both ends. Wash the apple and pear, and cut the carrots and fruit into large chunks.

**2** Press the ginger through a juicer, followed by the carrots, apple and pear. Stir the mixture to ensure all the juices are combined, and then pour into a large glass. Serve with a baby carrot stirrer, if liked, and drink immediately.

**Cook's Tip**

Carrots and apples make a great base for loads of juices and go well with both fruits and vegetables. Try ringing the changes by adding beet, orange, or tomato in place of the pear and ginger—or if you're feeling daring, try a combination of all three!

# Detox Indulger

One glass of this sweet, aromatic juice and you won't know what's hit you! Its luscious flavor belies its powerful detoxifying effects. Grapes, strawberries, and apples are all detox superfoods, cleansing the system and helping to flush out toxins.

**MAKES 1 GLASS**

1 papaya
4 large strawberries, hulled
½ cup/85g seedless red grapes
½ apple, roughly chopped
strawberries and grapes,
  to serve

1 Halve the papaya and use a teaspoon to scoop out the seeds. Cut the halves into wedges, then cut away and discard the skin. Halve the strawberries.

2 Press the papaya and strawberries through a juicer, followed by the grapes and apple. Stir and pour into a glass. Serve decorated with fresh strawberries and grapes.

# Rockmelon Cleanser

In natural medicine, mangoes are said to purify the blood, whereas fleshy melons are a great diuretic and help to cleanse the kidneys. Turmeric is a perfect partner to their sweet, aromatic juice and helps the body release toxins.

**MAKES 1 GLASS**

1 mango
¼ large rockmelon (about
  1lb/450g)
¼ tsp turmeric
2 tsp lemon juice

1 Using a small, sharp knife, remove the peel from the mango, then slice the flesh away from the pit. Scoop out the seeds from the melon, and then cut the fruit into slices. Remove the skin and cut the flesh into large chunks.

2 Press the mango through a juicer, followed by the melon, then stir in the turmeric and lemon juice. Pour into a glass and serve immediately.

Detox Indulger

Cherry-berry Clean-up

# Cherry-berry Clean-up

Grapes are great cleansers, and the darker the skin, the more potent their cleansing properties. However, they are often sprayed heavily with pesticides, so it is best to buy organic ones if you can. The juice has an intense flavor, so you'll probably want to dilute it with a little water and serve poured over ice.

**MAKES 1 SMALL GLASS**

⅔ cup/100g cherries
¼ cup/40g blueberries
½ cup/90g black or red grapes
2–3 tbsp water
Juice ¼ lime
Ice, to serve

1 Remove the pits from the cherries using a cherry-pitter, or halve and gently pull out the pit. Push the cherries, blueberries, and grapes through a juicer, and then dilute the juice with the water.

2 Add a squeeze of lime juice to taste, then pour the juice into an ice-filled glass and serve immediately. Garnish with extra cherries, if liked.

# Pear & Papaya Purifier

This gutsy juice is a good all-round cleanser and body fortifier. Pears help to flush out toxins, while papayas stimulate the digestive system and apricots strengthen the immune system. Gotu kola is thought to help reduce cellulite.

**MAKES 1 GLASS**

½ papaya
5 apricots
1 pear
¼ tsp gotu kola extract
2 tbsp water
Ice, to serve

1 Scoop out the seeds from the papaya, peel the fruit and chop the flesh into rough chunks. Cut around the crease of the apricots and twist the two sides apart and lever out the pit. Chop the pear.

2 Press the prepared fruit through a juicer, finishing with the pear. Stir in the gotu kola extract and water. Pour over ice and serve immediately.

# Pure & Peachy

This sweet, fruity juice tastes more like an indulgence that a penitential cleanser. Watermelons have a high water content, helping to flush out toxins from the system. For an extra hit of kidney-boosting potassium, leave the seeds in the fruit.

**MAKES 1 TALL GLASS**

2 peaches
9oz/250g watermelon
3 strawberries

**1** Place the peaches in a bowl, pour over boiling water and leave to stand for 30 seconds. Drain, then peel away the skins. Cut around the peach, and then twist the two sides apart and lever out the pit.

**2** Remove the rind from the watermelon, and then roughly chop all the fruit and place in a blender. Process for about 30 seconds until the mixture is smooth, and then pour into a glass and serve.

# Perfect Prunes

Sweet, toffee-colored and with barely a hint of aniseed, this luscious blend will help to deal with your toxic overload in a flash. Prunes are recommended for their laxative properties as well as their potent supply of antioxidants.

**MAKES 1 GLASS**

5 ready-to-eat dried prunes,
   pitted
½ cup/120ml boiling water
1 apple
¼ fennel bulb

**1** Place the prunes in a small bowl, pour over the boiling water and leave to soak overnight.

**2** Roughly chop the apple and fennel. Press the prunes through the juicer (reserving the soaking water), and then follow with the apples and fennel. Stir the reserved soaking water into the juice, and then pour into a glass and serve immediately.

Pure & Peachy

# The Juice Boost

Power juices to kick-start your system

Blackcurrant Beta-booster

# Blackcurrant Beta-booster

Packed with immune-boosting vitamin C, beta carotene, and body-building iron, this sweet, fruity juice is guaranteed to kick-start your whole system and keep it running at peak performance. Using cooked beet gives an intensely sweet juice, but you can use raw for a more potent-tasting juice.

**MAKES 1 GLASS**

2 cooked beets
1 apple
⅓ cup/60g blackcurrants, plus
  extra to garnish

**1** Roughly chop the beets and apple. Press the blackcurrants through a juicer followed by the chunks of beet and apple.

**2** Stir in about 2 tbsp cold water to dilute the juice, and then pour into a tall, ice-filled glass and serve garnished with blackcurrants.

> **Cook's Tip**
>
> When blackcurrants are out of season, you can use frozen berries instead. Leave them to thaw, then press through the juicer as you would fresh currants.

# Parsnip Sunshine

This glorious yellow juice, with its sweet, mild, refreshing flavor will put a spring in your step. Parsnips are great for the skin, hair, and nails, while bell peppers are a good source of vitamin C and excellent for boosting the immune system. Peppery radishes can help to clear the sinuses if you're feeling congested.

**MAKES 1 GLASS**

1¼ yellow bell peppers
¼ parsnip, trimmed
3 baby tomatoes, plus extra
  to garnish
6 radishes, trimmed

1 Halve the peppers and remove the seeds, white pith and stalk, then roughly chop the flesh. Roughly chop the parsnip.

2 Press the tomatoes, radishes, and parsnip through the juicer, followed by the bell peppers. Stir the juice, then pour into a glass. Spike several baby tomatoes on a skewer, and add to the juice.

# Fierce & Fiery Butternut

This intensely sweet, fiery hot juice is guaranteed to blow out the cobwebs. Try to find Thai chilies—their intense, ferocious heat contrasts wonderfully with the thick, syrupy butternut squash juice.

**MAKES 1 SMALL GLASS**

1 small green chili
1⅔ cups/240g butternut squash
¾ pear

1 Remove the seeds and white pith from the chili, and then mince finely and set aside. Peel the squash and roughly chop the flesh. Roughly chop the pear.

2 Press the squash and pear through a juicer, and then whisk in the chili and pour into a small glass.

Parsnip Sunshine

Sweet Pea

# Sweet Pea

Fresh, young peas are packed with nutrients, and this luscious, minty concoction has all kinds of health benefits. Mint is great for the digestion, cucumber is good for healthy hair and nails, and grapes help to cleanse the whole system.

MAKES 1 SMALL GLASS

¼ cucumber
2 tbsp chopped fresh mint,
  plus mint leaves to garnish
⅔ cup/100g shelled peas
½ cup/90g white grapes

1 Roughly chop the cucumber. Press the mint through the juicer, followed by half the cucumber.

2 Push through the peas, followed by the remaining cucumber and the grapes. Stir the juice, pour into a glass and serve immediately.

# Full of Beans

You'll be jumping with energy and good health after a glass of this mild, tangy, beany juice spiked with immune-boosting echinacea. Sprouted beans are high in valuable vitamins and minerals, while bell peppers are packed with immune-boosting beta carotene and vitamin C, and celery helps to keep the liver and gall bladder healthy.

MAKES 1 GLASS

½ red bell pepper
¾ yellow bell pepper
1½ cups/135g mung bean
  sprouts
1 stick celery
¼ teaspoon echinacea

1 Remove the seeds, pith, and stalks from the peppers and roughly chop the flesh. Press the bean sprouts, celery, and bell peppers through a juicer.

2 Stir the echinacea into the juice, pour into a glass and serve immediately.

# Red Cabbage Riot

Red cabbage and cumin are classic partners and offer a powerhouse of nutrients. The cabbage is packed with disease-fighting phytochemicals and vitamins, while cumin is considered to be a potent, antioxidant super-spice. Drink the juice immediately: if left to stand the cabbage flavor intensifies and becomes unpleasant.

**MAKES 1 SMALL GLASS**

½ tsp cumin seeds
1¼ cups/150g red cabbage
½ beet
⅓ cup/30g broccoli florets
¼ pear, plus extra wedges
  to serve

1 Place the cumin seeds in a mortar and crush with a pestle. Add 1½ tbsp boiling water and steep for 5 minutes. Meanwhile, chop the cabbage and beet.

2 Strain the cumin infusion, reserving the juice and discarding the seeds. Press the vegetables and pear through a juicer, and then stir the cumin infusion into the juice, pour into a glass, garnish with a wedge of pear and drink immediately.

# Asian Go-juice

You need only a small shot of this potent, peppery juice. Asian bok choy has a mild, sweet, slightly peppery flavor and is packed with nutrients, including carotenoids. Garlic and chili are both immune boosters, and give this juice its distinctive flavor.

**MAKES 1 SMALL GLASS**

1 red Thai chili
5½oz/150g bok choy
1 garlic clove, peeled
¼ cup/45g white grapes
Juice ¼ lime

1 Finely chop the chili and set aside. Roughly chop the bok choy. Press the garlic through a juicer, followed by the bok choy and grapes.

2 Squeeze in the lime juice, and then stir in chopped chili. Pour into a shot glass and serve.

Red Cabbage Riot

Spicy Avocado Blitz

# Spicy Avocado Blitz

When you haven't got time to stop for lunch, grab a glassful of this rich, creamy, energizing blend instead. The natural fructose in the oranges will give you an instant energy boost, while the avocado will provide a source of sustained energy.

**MAKES 1 LARGE GLASS**

½ avocado
2½ oranges
¼ cup/60ml water
1 green chili, seeded and finely
    chopped
Red chili, to decorate

**1** Scoop the flesh from the avocado, chop it roughly and place in a blender. Squeeze the juice from the oranges, and then add to the avocado with the water and green chili. Blend until smooth and creamy, adding a little more water if necessary.

**2** Pour the smoothie into a tall glass, decorate with fresh red chili—either shredded or whole—and serve.

# Green Tea Temptation

Enjoy this mild, creamy blend for breakfast, and it will provide sustained energy right through until lunchtime. Apricots and almonds are both immune boosters, and green tea is rich in anti-viral properties that can help stave off illness.

**MAKES 1 LARGE GLASS**

1 tsp green tea
1 cup/240ml boiling water
¼ cup/50g dried apricots
2 tbsp ground almonds
1 tsp lemon juice
½ tsp clear honey

**1** Place the green tea leaves in a pitcher and pour over the boiling water. Leave to steep for 5 minutes, and then strain over the apricots. Soak overnight.

**2** Place the ground almonds in a blender and add the apricots and green tea, lemon juice and honey. Blend for 1–2 minutes until smooth and creamy, and then pour into a glass and serve.

# Tropical Glow

**This mild yet astringent juice is great for the digestive system. Papain from the pineapples and papaya helps to digest protein, and carrots are real immune-boosters.**

**MAKES 1 LARGE GLASS**

½ large papaya
¼ large pineapple (about 9oz/250g), plus extra to decorate
1 large carrot, trimmed

1 Scoop out the seeds from the papaya, then cut the flesh into wedges and remove the skin. Cut off the skin from the pineapple and discard, then cut the flesh away from the central core and discard the core. Cut the carrot into rough chunks.

2 Press the papaya through a juicer, followed by the pineapple and carrot. Stir the juice, pour into a tall glass, add a wedge of pineapple and serve.

# Asparagus & Berry Tingler

**Green asparagus and crunchy apples are great for boosting the urinary and digestive systems, while strawberries offer an extra does of vitamin C, which is essential for glowing good health and a strong immune system.**

**MAKES 1 SMALL GLASS**

5 strawberries
¼ pear
1 apple
1¾oz/50g asparagus
about 3 tbsp water
Juice ¼ lemon
Ice, to serve

1 Halve any large strawberries, and roughly chop the pear and apple. Press the strawberries though a juicer followed by the asparagus, pear, and apple.

2 Dilute the juice with water, then add a squeeze of lemon juice to taste. Pour into a glass filled with ice, and serve immediately.

Tropical Glow

Berry Bright Eyes

# Berry Bright Eyes

This sweet, intensely flavored juice starts by waking up your taste buds before kick-starting the rest of your body. Packed with nutrients, this juice is particularly good for the eyes and for boosting the immune system. It's also an effective cleanser, so is the perfect choice if you want to improve the functioning of your whole system.

**MAKES 1 GLASS**

3 strawberries
1 pear
¼ cup/35g raspberries
¼ cup/40g blueberries
Ice, to serve
Berries, to decorate (optional)

1 Halve any large strawberries and roughly chop the pear into large chunks.

2 Press the berries through the juicer, followed by the chunks of pear, and then pour into a glass filled with ice. Decorate with a few extra berries, if liked, and serve immediately.

**Cook's Tip**

This sweet, fruity juice makes a fabulous non-alcoholic cocktail for a special occasion. Or even better, combine it with champagne or sparkling wine for a sophisticated summery alternative to the classic Buck's Fizz.

# Citrus Sizzler

Tantalizingly tangy and refreshing, this juice is full of vitamin C, which is essential for good health—helping to boost your immune system, maintain healthy bones, and aid recuperation from illness. It also helps your body to absorb iron, helping you to feel fit, healthy, and alert. Make a big jug for breakfast as a treat for the family!

**MAKES 1 TALL GLASS**

2 oranges
½ pink grapefruit
¼ lime, plus lime slices or
   wedges, to decorate
Ice, to serve

1 Halve the oranges. Using a citrus squeezer, squeeze out the juice from the oranges and grapefruit, and then squeeze in the lime juice.

2 If you prefer a smooth juice, strain the juice through a fine sieve. Fill a glass with ice, pour in the juice and decorate with lime wedges.

# Melon Magic

Fruity and refreshing, this mild, melony smoothie is just the thing when you need a quick energy boost. Fresh apricots are in season for only a short time, but you can use dried apricots instead; simply soak in water for a few hours until they plump up.

**MAKES 1 GLASS**

⅛ Ogen melon
3 apricots
1 tbsp pumpkin seeds
¼ tsp ginkgo biloba extract
2–3 tbsp water

1 Scoop out the melon seeds and discard, then scoop the flesh into a blender. Cut around the crease in the apricots, and then twist the two halves apart and lever out the pits. Roughly chop the flesh and place in the blender.

2 Add the pumpkin seeds and ginkgo biloba extract and blend for about 1 minute to make a smooth purée. Stir in a little water and serve in a tall glass.

Citrus Sizzler

Passionate Protector

# Passionate Protector

This tangy, fragrant, refreshing juice is packed with immune-boosting beta carotene to protect against ill-health, and is also great for healthy skin and eyes.

**MAKES 1 LARGE GLASS**

2 passion fruit, plus extra
  to garnish
2 carrots, trimmed
1 orange

1 Halve the passion fruits and scoop the pulp into a sieve placed over a pitcher. Using the back of a spoon, press the pulp into the pitcher.

2 Cut the carrot into rough chunks. Peel the orange and divide into quarters, then press the orange and carrots through a juicer. Stir the juice into the passion fruit pulp. Pour into a tall glass, decorate with a wedge of passionfruit, and drink immediately.

# Nectarine Nurture

This fruity, nutty smoothie is jam-packed with nutrients to get your body in tip-top condition. Red grapes contain resveratrol, a potent antioxidant, while wheat germ and cashew nuts provide B vitamins, iron and vitamin E.

**MAKES 1 TALL GLASS**

2 nectarines
1 tbsp cashew nuts
1 tbsp wheat germ
1 cup red grapes

1 Cut around the crease of the nectarines, twist apart, then lever out the pits. Chop the flesh and place in a blender with the nuts and wheat germ.

2 Press the grapes through the juicer, then pour the juice into the blender and process for 2 minutes, scraping down the sides once or twice, until the mixture is smooth and creamy. Pour into a glass and serve immediately.

# Vital Vigour

Instant energizers

# Tomato Pep

Traditionally, basil has been credited with being a relaxing herb, but teamed with get-up-and-go tomatoes and other stimulating herbs, it helps to make a delicious, invigorating juice. Baby tomatoes have a particularly sweet, intense flavor, but you can use ordinary tomatoes if you prefer.

**MAKES 1 SMALL GLASS**

½ apple
1 sprig fresh thyme, plus extra
  to decorate
1½ tbsp chopped fresh basil
1 tsp chopped fresh mint
1½ cups/250g baby tomatoes

**1** Roughly chop the apple and strip the leaves off the thyme sprig. Press the herbs through a juicer followed by the apple, then press through the tomatoes. (Be careful as the baby tomatoes have a tendency to shoot back out of some juicers!)

**2** Stir the juice, pour into a glass, decorate with basil leaves and serve immediately.

# Brazen Brassicas

The brassica family, which includes broccoli and spinach, offers a wealth of nutrients. Here, they are combined in a surprisingly creamy, mild juice, which is full of vitamin C, iron, and beta carotene and will protect your whole system.

**MAKES 1 GLASS**

3½oz/100g broccoli
1 orange
2 cups/70g baby spinach
1 celery stick
1 tsp kelp

**1** Roughly chop the broccoli, and then peel the orange and divide the flesh into segments.

**2** Press the spinach through a juicer, followed by the celery, broccoli, and, finally, the orange. Stir the kelp into the juice, then pour into a glass and serve.

Tomato Pep

Green Horsepower

# Green Horsepower

Peppery horseradish adds a hot dimension to this surprisingly mild, sweet juice and helps to clear the sinuses if you're feeling congested. Sugary apples offer an instant energy hit, whereas leafy green spinach and broccoli contain anti-oxidants to boost your immune system. Spinach also contains zeaxanthin and lutein, which are thought to protect the eyes against ageing.

**MAKES 1 GLASS**

5½oz/150g broccoli
1½ apples
3 cups/120g baby spinach
¾ tsp grated horseradish

1 Roughly chop the broccoli and apples. Press the spinach leaves through a juicer, followed by the broccoli and apples.

2 Stir the grated horseradish into the juice, pour into a glass and serve immediately.

### Cook's Tip

You can alter the proportions of broccoli and spinach if you like. They both produce wonderfully mild juices—and are equally beneficial to your health. And if you prefer a pepper-free juice, you can leave out the horseradish too.

# Beta-C Bonanza

Strangely, this energizing blend of vegetables and pineapple has a definite hint of strawberries. The natural fruit sugars give a great energy boost, while hefty doses of beta carotene, vitamin C, and other health-giving nutrients and phytochemicals will have you firing on all cylinders in no time.

**MAKES 1 TALL GLASS**

1 red bell pepper
¼ large pineapple (about
  1lb/450g)
¼ beet, scrubbed

1 Cut the pepper in half, remove the seeds and white pith, and then cut the flesh into chunks. Cut the skin from the pineapple, and then remove the core and cut the flesh into rough chunks.

2 Press the bell pepper, pineapple, and beet through the juicer, then pour into a glass and serve.

# Cauliflower Tingler

Cauliflower contains immune-boosting antioxidants and is the richest source of vitamin K, essential for healthy bones, wound repair and blood clotting so it makes a useful addition to healthy juices. Zingy pineapple is the perfect partner, masking the rather strong flavor of the cauliflower juice. Use a small, sweet cauliflower.

**MAKES 1 GLASS**

4½oz/130g cauliflower
5½oz/150g pineapple

1 Cut the cauliflower into florets. Remove the skin from the pineapple and roughly chop the flesh, discarding the tough central core.

2 Press the cauliflower through the juicer, followed by the pineapple. Stir the juice, pour into a glass and serve immediately.

Beta-C Bonanza

Minty Minx

# Minty Minx

Tantalizingly tangy and refreshingly minty, this luscious green juice will start by tempting your taste buds before moving on to the rest of your body. Packed with invigorating vitamins and soothing mint, this is a great juice to sip first thing.

**MAKES 1 GLASS**

1 kiwi fruit
1 orange
1 apple
½ cup/15g fresh mint leaves,
  plus extra to decorate
Ice, to serve (optional)

**1** Peel the kiwi fruit and orange, and then roughly chop all the fruit. Press the mint leaves through a juicer followed by the kiwi fruit, orange and apple.

**2** Stir the juice, and then pour into a tall glass. Add a few ice cubes, if you like, and decorate with mint.

# Veggie Revitalizer

Give yourself an energy boost with this sweet, sharp, tangy blend, pepped up with spicy ginger. Packed with health-giving nutrients, including vitamin C, beta carotene, and lycopene, it offers your body fuel and protection.

**MAKES 1 TALL GLASS**

½in/1cm fresh root ginger
1 kiwi fruit
5½oz/150g butternut squash
¼ cup/40g green grapes
5 tomatoes, roughly chopped

**1** Using a sharp knife, cut off the skin from the ginger. Peel the kiwi fruit and cut the flesh into rough chunks. Remove the skin from the butternut squash and roughly chop the flesh.

**2** Press the ginger through the juicer followed by the kiwi fruit and squash, then push through the grapes and tomatoes. Stir the juice to combine, and then pour into a glass and serve.

# Guarana Get-go

**Guarana was originally discovered by the indigenous people of the Brazilian rainforest. It has amazing natural powers, providing sustained energy.**

**MAKES 1 TALL GLASS**

2 ripe plums, plus 1 extra
 to serve
2 oranges
¼ cup/30g raspberries
¼ tsp guarana extract
¼–½ tsp clear honey (optional)

1 Cut all the way around the plum, through the crease, then twist apart and lever out the pit. Cut the flesh into large chunks.

2 Peel the oranges and divide the flesh into large chunks. Press the raspberries through a juicer (reserving one or two for decoration), followed by the plums and oranges. Stir in the guarana extract and a little honey, to taste. Pour into a glass and decorate with the raspberries and wedges of plum.

# Brewer's Breakfast

**Packed with apricots, banana, and apples, this creamy smoothie provides a great source of energy. Brewer's yeast is rich in B vitamins, iron, zinc and magnesium.**

**MAKES 1 TALL GLASS**

2 apples
5 apricots
1 banana
1 tbsp brewer's yeast

1 Roughly chop the apples and press through a juicer. Pour the juice into a blender. Cut around the crease of the apricots, twist the two halves apart and lever out the pits. Add the apricots to the juice.

2 Peel the banana, cut into chunks and add to the blender with the brewer's yeast. Blend until smooth and creamy, pour into a glass and serve.

Guarana Get-go

Mango Reviver

# Mango Reviver

**Perfect for breakfast, or as a pick-me-up later in the day, this thick, fragrant blend is packed with vitamin C, beta carotene, and natural sugars to give you instant energy.**

**MAKES 1 LARGE GLASS**

½ mango
1 cup/125g strawberries, hulled
2 small dessert apples
Small strawberries, to
  decorate

1 Cut the mango flesh away from the pit, and slice off the skin. Place the mango and strawberries in a blender, reserving a wedge of mango for decoration.

2 Cut the apples into large chunks, and then press through a juicer. Pour the juice over the fruit and blend until smooth and creamy.

3 Spike the strawberries and mango on a bamboo skewer, and then pour the smoothie into a large glass. Add the fruit skewer and serve immediately.

# Tropical Trembler

**Fragrant mango, zingy pineapple and zesty lime juice combine to make an enlivening tropical juice-boost. Packed with vitamins and phytochemicals, this makes a perfect breakfast juice, or pick-me-up after work when you just need to keep going.**

**MAKES 1 GLASS**

1½in/4cm slice pineapple
  (about 12oz/350g)
½ mango
1 satsuma
1½ tsp lime juice

1 Cut the skin off the pineapple, and then remove the central core and roughly chop the flesh. Peel the mango and roughly chop the flesh.

2 Press the mango through the juicer, followed by the satsuma and pineapple, and then stir in the lime juice, pour into a glass and serve immediately.

# Poppy Seed Pep

**One glass of this tantalizing combination of tropical fruits and raspberries, packed with vitamin C and B vitamins and you'll be zipping about in no time.**

MAKES 1 GLASS

½ papaya
2 kiwi fruits
8oz/225g pineapple
¼ cup/30g raspberries, plus
   extra to decorate
½ tsp poppy seeds

**1** Scoop out the seeds from the papaya and discard. Cut the flesh into wedges, then cut off the skin. Peel the kiwi fruits and chop the flesh roughly. Cut the skin away from the pineapple, remove the central core and chop the flesh roughly.

**2** Press the papaya, raspberries, kiwi fruits, and pineapple through a juicer. Stir the poppy seeds into the juice, then pour into a tall glass, decorate with raspberries and serve immediately.

# Vitamin-C Zing

**Wake up and get going with this fresh and zingy-tasting juice. It offers instant energy, essential health-promoting nutrients, and fabulous flavor.**

MAKES 1 TALL GLASS

2 carrots, trimmed
1 kiwi fruit
½ yellow bell pepper
1in/2.5cm slice fresh root
   ginger
1 tbsp chopped fresh parsley
juice ¼ lemon

**1** Chop the carrots roughly. Peel the kiwi fruit and quarter them. Remove the seeds from the bell pepper and roughly chop the flesh.

**2** Press the ginger and parsley through a juicer, followed by the carrots, kiwi fruit, and pepper. Stir the juice, squeeze in lemon juice to taste, then pour into a glass and serve immediately.

Poppy Seed Pep

Pomegranate & Watermelon Juice

# Pomegranate & Watermelon Juice

**This long, cool, and refreshing drink is perfect for a hot summer day. Dehydration can make you feel tired and lethargic, so make sure you keep your fluid and energy levels up by sipping this sweet, fruity drink.**

**MAKES 1 LARGE GLASS**

½ pomegranate
1lb 3oz/550g slice watermelon
½–1 tsp lime juice
Pomegranate seeds,
  to decorate
Ice, to serve

1 Using a teaspoon, scoop the pomegranate seeds into a sieve placed over a pitcher (reserving a few seeds for decoration). Press the seeds with the back of the spoon to extract all the juice, and then discard the seeds in the sieve.

2 Cut the rind from the watermelon and cut the flesh into rough chunks. Press the watermelon through a juicer, and then add the melon juice to the pomegranate juice. Stir in the lime juice to taste, pour into a tall glass filled with ice, and decorate with pomegranate seeds.

## Cook's Tip

If you're having problems removing the pomegranate seeds, tap the fruit with the flat back of a wooden spoon. The seeds should pop right out, into the sieve. Press the skin inside out to remove any remaining seeds.

# Watermelon Marvel

Sweet, fruity, and unbelievably good for you, this refreshing juice will give you instant energy. Blueberries are an immune booster and, combined with cranberries, are an excellent natural remedy for urinary tract infections. Watermelons contain lycopene, which is thought to help fight cancer.

**MAKES 1 GLASS**

1lb 1oz/475g watermelon
80g/½ cup blueberries
80g/½ cup cranberries
Extra berries, to decorate

1 Cut the rind from the watermelon and cut the flesh into large chunks. Press the berries through a juicer, followed by the watermelon.

2 Pour the juice into a tall glass, decorate with extra berries and serve immediately.

# Cheeky Cherry

This sweet, sharp, slightly astringent juice will have you up and buzzing in no time. Cherries and pears will boost your energy levels, and strawberries also contain valuable B vitamins. To make a cleansing variation with a slightly milder flavor, try using a large wedge of rockmelon in place of the pear.

**MAKES 1 SMALL GLASS**

½ cup/80g cherries
5 strawberries, hulled
1 pear, roughly chopped

1 Remove the stalks and pits from the cherries. (If you don't have a cherry-pitter, cut around the crease of the cherries, gently prize the two halves apart and pull out the pit.)

2 Cut any large strawberries in half, then push all the fruit through a juicer. Stir, then pour the juice into a small glass and sip slowly.

Watermelon Marvel

# Chill Out

Calming Soothers

Fennel Lull

# Fennel Lull

Calm down at the end of a busy day with a tall glass of this milky, soothing blend. Fennel gives the juice a faint hint of aniseed and is also believed to have a calming, restful effect on the body. In traditional medicine, it is often recommended as a remedy for headaches and migraine.

**MAKES 1 LARGE GLASS**

1½ fennel bulbs
3in/7.5cm chunk of cucumber

1 Cut the fennel and cucumber into rough chunks, and then press them through a juicer.

2 Stir, then pour into a tall glass, decorate with wedges of cucumber or fennel, and sip slowly.

# Minty Salad Juice

This unusual combination of flavors makes a delicious, soothing juice with a bitter tang. Lettuce, celery, and mint are renowned for their calming properties and are even thought to combat insomnia.

**MAKES 1 GLASS**

¼ iceberg lettuce
½ pink grapefruit
1 celery stick
1 tsp finely chopped mint, plus mint leaves, to decorate
Crushed ice, to serve

1 Roughly chop the lettuce. Remove the peel from the grapefruit and divide the flesh into segments. Press the lettuce, grapefruit, and celery through a juicer, then stir the mint into the juice.

2 Fill a glass with crushed ice, then pour over the juice and decorate with mint leaves. (If you prefer a smooth juice, leave the juice to absorb the minty flavor for 10 minutes, then strain into the glass.)

# Cardamom Calmer

Asparagus is well known for its calming properties, and is said to promote sleep. Fragrant cardamom, a digestive soother, adds a subtle, warm spice to the juice and the yellow peppers provide vitamin C, which is lost from the body in times of stress.

**MAKES 1 GLASS**

1½ tsp cardamom pods
¼ cup/60ml water
1½ yellow bell peppers
⅓ pear
3½oz/100g asparagus

**1** Place the cardamom pods in a mortar and crush them lightly with a pestle. Tip into a small pan, add the water and bring to the boil. Reduce the heat to very low and simmer for 3 minutes. Remove the pan from the heat and leave to stand for 10 minutes.

**2** Meanwhile, halve the bell peppers, remove the seeds, white pith, and stalk, and roughly chop the flesh. Roughly chop the pear. Press the asparagus through a juicer, followed by the peppers and pear. Strain the cardamom soaking water into the juice and stir. Pour the juice into a glass and serve.

# Cucumber Chill-out

Grapes and mint are both used as traditional calmers, helping to relax the body and mind. The combination of cucumber and grapes is particularly mild and mellow.

**MAKES 1 GLASS**

½ cucumber, peeled
1 cup/90g white grapes
1 tbsp chopped mint

**1** Roughly chop the cucumber and push it through a juicer with the grapes.

**2** Pour the juice into a blender, add the mint, and process briefly until the mint is finely chopped. Pour into a glass and serve immediately.

Cardamom Calmer

**Broccoli Booster**

# Broccoli Booster

This restorative blend spiced up with peppery rocket is sure to calm you down and make you feel like your old self in no time. Mood-enhancing broccoli and orange blend perfectly with calming celery to make a sweet, pungent juice.

**MAKES 1 GLASS**

2 oranges
1½oz/40g broccoli
1½ cups/45g arugula
½ stick celery

**1** Peel the oranges and divide into large segments. Break the broccoli into small florets. Press the rocket through a juicer, followed by the broccoli, oranges, and celery.

**2** Give the juice a stir, pour into a glass, decorate with an arugula leaf, if liked, and serve immediately.

# Cinnamon Roots

Sweet, warmly spiced and utterly refreshing, this calming blend practically forces you to take a step back and chill out. Cinnamon and cucumber help to soothe the system, while the boost of beta carotene from the orange vegetables will help to protect the body while your defenses are down.

**MAKES 1 GLASS**

1 cinnamon stick
½ cup/120ml boiling water
3oz/75g sweet potato, peeled
3oz/75g butternut squash, peeled
1 carrot, trimmed
2in/5cm slice of cucumber

**1** Put the cinnamon stick and water in a small pan, bring to the boil, and then simmer gently for about 5 minutes. Remove from the heat and leave to cool for 10 minutes. Remove the cinnamon stick.

**2** Roughly chop the vegetables, and then press them through a juicer. Stir in the cinnamon water, pour into a tall glass and serve.

# Beet & Orange Smoothie

A vegetable smoothie may seem like an odd idea but it's so good and offers the perfect combination for relaxation and restoration. Beet is a natural restorative and blood-builder, while yogurt is naturally soothing and calming.

**MAKES 1 GLASS**

1 cooked beet
2 oranges
¼ cup/60ml live plain yogurt

1 Roughly chop the beet, then peel the oranges and divide into chunks. Press the beet through the juicer, followed by the oranges.

2 Reserve about half the juice, then add the yogurt to the remaining juice and stir until well-blended. Pour the yogurt mixture into a glass, then carefully pour the reserved juice over the back of a spoon so that it floats on top of the smoothie. Serve.

# Molasses Tranquillizer

Sweet and delicious, this creamy blend is perfect for chilling out with. Rich in B-vitamins, which play an important role in the body's ability to cope with stress, this luscious smoothie will also help to battle insomnia and improve your mood.

**MAKES 1 GLASS**

4 dates, chopped
1 tbsp linseeds
3 tbsp boiling water
¾ cup/180ml live plain yogurt
½ tsp molasses
Juice ¼ lemon

1 Put the dates and linseeds in a bowl and pour over the boiling water. Leave to stand for 30 minutes.

2 Tip the dates, seeds and soaking liquid into a blender and add the yogurt and molasses. Blend for about 2 minutes until smooth and creamy, then squeeze in the lemon juice and blitz briefly to combine. Pour into a glass and serve immediately.

Beet & Orange Smoothie

Creamy Avocado Relaxer

# Creamy Avocado Relaxer

One sip of this glorious smoothie and you won't care about the good it's doing your body—you'll just want to indulge yourself in its gorgeous taste and texture. The avocado gives the smoothie a wonderfully rich consistency, while the grapes, which are used in traditional medicine for their calming, restful properties, will help you to chill out and relax. Avocado has the added bonus of being great for your skin so you'll end up looking gorgeous, as well as chilled-out!

**MAKES 1 TALL GLASS**

1 pear
¾ cup/150g white grapes
¼ avocado
½ lime

**1** Roughly chop the pear, then press through a juicer with the grapes. Pour the juice into a blender.

**2** Scoop the avocado flesh from the skin, chop roughly and add to the juice in the blender. Blend until smooth and creamy.

**3** Stir in lime juice to taste, then pour the smoothie into a tall glass and serve immediately.

### Cook's Tip

The flesh of avocado oxidizes and discolors when exposed to the air. To prevent any leftover avocado turning brown, squeeze lemon juice over the exposed flesh and cover tightly with clear film. Use within 1 or 2 days.

# Magical Mellow-out

Sip this fabulously creamy, frothy smoothie at the end of a long, hard day and feel your mood pick up almost immediately. Bananas, peanut butter, wheat germ, and soya milk all contain nutrients that help to calm and lift the spirits—making this a perfect chill-out drink when you need to escape from your hectic schedule.

**MAKES 1 LARGE GLASS**

1 ripe banana
1½ tbsp peanut butter
1 tbsp wheat germ
1 tsp clear honey
1 cup/240ml soya milk

**1** Peel the banana and break it into large chunks, then put in a blender with the peanut butter, wheat germ, honey and soya milk.

**2** Blend for about 1 minute until smooth and frothy. Pour into a tall glass and sip slowly.

# Lemon Balm Calm

The herb lemon balm is a traditional calming remedy and is said to promote sleep. Paired with the mellow flavor of sweet melon and vitamin-C rich orange, this juice is guaranteed to help you relax and restore your body to its natural equilibrium.

**MAKES 1 GLASS**

½ Ogen melon
1 orange
½ tsp chopped lemon balm
Ice, to serve

**1** Scoop out the seeds from the melon, remove the rind, then roughly chop the flesh. Peel the orange and divide into several segments. Press the fruit through a juicer.

**2** Put the lemon balm into a mortar and crush lightly with a pestle to release some of the aroma, and then tip the lightly crushed herb into a glass filled with ice. Pour over the juice and serve.

Magical Mellow-out

Fig-tastic Oat Soother

# Fig-tastic Oat Soother

Chill out and unwind after a hard day with this thick, creamy confection. Oats are a traditional calmer, and soya milk contains amino acids that are converted into the mood-enhancing chemical, serotonin.

**MAKES 1 LARGE GLASS**

2 tbsp rolled oats
¼ cup/60ml boiling water
6 ready-to-eat dried figs
1 cup/240ml soya milk
1 tsp lemon juice

**1** Put the oats in a bowl, pour over the boiling water and leave to stand for 10 minutes.

**2** Meanwhile, remove the woody stems from the figs and discard. Chop the figs and place them in a blender. Pour in the soya milk and lemon juice, and then add the soaked oats and any remaining liquid.

**3** Blend until smooth and creamy, then pour the mixture into a glass and serve with a spoon.

# Chamomile Quietener

Fragrant chamomile, with its apple-like scent, is known for its calming, soporific properties and makes a fabulous base for this sweet, sumptuous smoothie.

**MAKES 1 GLASS**

1 tsp dried chamomile flowers
¾ cup/180ml boiling water
2 ripe figs
¾ cup/115g blueberries
1 tsp clear honey
1 tsp lemon juice

**1** Put the chamomile in a pitcher and pour over the boiling water. Leave to steep for 5 minutes, then strain and leave to cool. Discard the flowers.

**2** Halve the figs, then scoop the flesh into a blender and add the blueberries and honey. Pour over the cooled chamomile water and blend until smooth. Stir in the lemon juice, pour over ice and serve.

# Lavender & Watermelon Wind-down

**Fragrant lavender is known for it's calming properties, and it is also said to help relieve headaches. It adds a distinctive depth of flavor to this sweet, fruity juice, making a refreshing, relaxing drink to sip after a hectic day at work.**

**MAKES 1 GLASS**

½ tsp lavender flowers
¼ cup/60ml boiling water
12oz/350g watermelon
½ cup/90g red grapes
Lavender stalks, to decorate

**1** Put the lavender in a small bowl and pour over the boiling water. Leave to stand for about 10 minutes, then strain the flavored water into a pitcher and discard the flowers.

**2** Meanwhile, cut the rind from the watermelon and cut the flesh into large chunks. Press the watermelon through a juicer, followed by the red grapes, then stir in the lavender water.

**3** Pour the juice into a glass, decorate with the lavender stalks and serve immediately.

> **Cook's Tip**
>
> When lavender is out of season, you can use dried lavender flowers instead. They are available from most health food stores and can be used in exactly the same way as the fresh flowers.

Lavender & Watermelon Wind-down

Nutty Plum Smoothie

# Nutty Plum Smoothie

Sweet, tart, and utterly moreish, this smoothie is the perfect chill-out blend. Nuts and seeds are rich in B vitamins, which help the body to cope in times of stress, while sesame seeds are a good source of magnesium, which is lost from the body during stressful situations.

**MAKES 1 TALL GLASS**

2 plums
¼ cup/35g raspberries
1 tbsp ground almonds
1 tbsp sesame seeds
¼ cup/60ml water

1 Cut around the crease of the plums, then twist apart and lever out the pit. Roughly chop the flesh.

2 Place the chopped plums in a blender with the raspberries, ground almonds, sesame seeds, and water, and blend for about 1 minute until smooth and creamy. Pour the smoothie into a glass and serve.

# Blackberry Spice

Soothing cinnamon is a traditional remedy for easing an upset stomach and makes the perfect partner to blackberries, which are said to calm the nervous system. This delectable juice is like a slice of pie in a glass: utterly delicious!

**MAKES 1 LARGE GLASS**

1 cinnamon stick
½ cup/120ml boiling water
1½ well-flavored dessert apples
½ cup/75g blackberries

1 Put the cinnamon and boiling water in a small pan, bring to the boil, and then simmer gently for about 5 minutes. Leave to cool for 10 minutes. Remove and reserve the cinnamon stick.

2 Roughly chop the apples. Press the blackberries through a juicer, followed by the apples, and then stir the cooled cinnamon water into the juice. Pour into a glass and serve with the cinnamon stick.

**5**

# In The Comfort Zone

Miraculous mood-enhancers

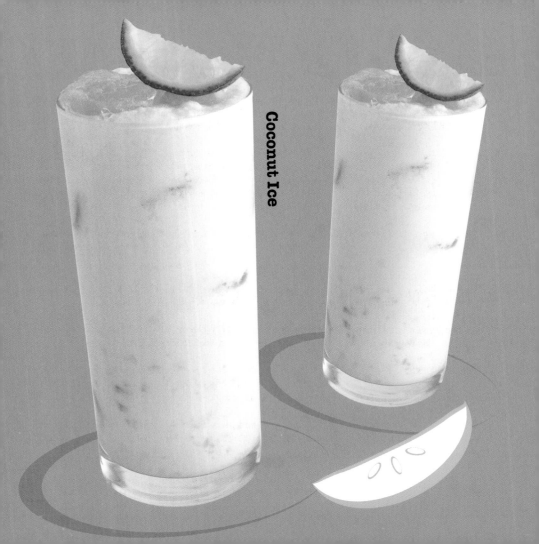

Coconut Ice

# Coconut Ice

Bringing together the classic Thai flavors of coconut, ginger, and lime juice, this creamy, tangy blend is utterly divine. Feelings of well-being will pervade your body after just one sip. Ginger is a traditional remedy for depression.

**MAKES 1 GLASS**

1 piece stem ginger in syrup,
  plus 2 tsp syrup from the jar
¾ cup/180ml coconut milk
½ lime
Lime rind, to decorate
Crushed ice, to serve

1 Finely chop the stem ginger, then place in a blender with the coconut milk and ginger syrup. Squeeze in the juice from the lime. Blend very briefly to combine. (Literally just give it one blitz because overblending will cause the mixture will separate.)

2 Fill a tall glass with crushed ice and pour over the smoothie. Decorate with the lime zest and serve.

# Nutty Nutmeg Smoothie

It's hard to believe that this rich, creamy blend is dairy-free. With its luxurious texture and sweet, warmly spiced flavor, it feels like the ultimate indulgence.

**MAKES 1 LARGE GLASS**

Scant ¼ cup/25g cashew nuts
2 oranges
2 tbsp/30g chopped dates
½ cup/120ml soya milk
¼ tsp freshly grated nutmeg

1 Place the nuts in a food processor. Squeeze the juice from one of the oranges and add to the nuts. Process for about 1 minute until smooth.

2 Squeeze the juice from the second orange and add to the nut mixture with the dates. Process for a further 1–2 minutes until smooth.

3 Add the soya milk and nutmeg and process to combine. Pour the mixture into a glass and serve.

# Serotonin Smoothie

**Bananas are a great energy booster, so if you've got a blood-sugar low, this mild, creamy blend will give you a real lift. Bananas and soya milk also contain the amino acid tryptophan, which is converted into the mood-enhancing chemical, serotonin.**

**MAKES 1 LARGE GLASS**

1 banana
1 cup/125g strawberries, hulled
½ cup/120ml soya milk

1 Peel the banana and cut into big chunks. Place in a blender with the strawberries and soya milk.

2 Process for about 30 seconds until smooth and creamy, then pour into a glass and serve.

# De-stress Juice

**Pineapples and kiwi fruit are rich in vitamin C, which is a valuable anti-stress nutrient, making this the perfect juice when you want to sit back, relax and indulge yourself. For a truly luxurious treat, add a scoop of frozen yogurt.**

**MAKES 1 GLASS**

1 kiwi fruit
1in/2½cm slice pineapple
9oz/250g watermelon
Lemon juice, to taste

1 Peel the kiwi fruit and cut into rough chunks. Remove the skin and central core from the pineapple and cut the flesh into rough chunks. Remove the rind from the watermelon and cut the flesh into rough chunks.

2 Press the fruit through a juicer, and then stir in a little lemon juice to taste. Pour into a glass and serve immediately.

Serotonin Smoothie

Apricot Sweetie

# Apricot Sweetie

Dried apricots give you a great iron-boost, which helps with the production of feel-good chemicals in the brain, while sunflower seeds are rich in B vitamins, which help your body to cope with stressful situations.

**MAKES 1 TALL GLASS**

¼ cup/50g ready-to-eat dried apricots
1 tbsp sunflower seeds
⅔ cup/160ml live plain yogurt
⅓ cup/80ml milk
1 tsp clear honey
2 tsp lemon juice

1 Roughly chop the apricots and put in a blender with the sunflower seeds, yogurt, milk, honey, and lemon juice.

2 Blend the ingredients together for 1–2 minutes until really smooth and creamy. Pour into a glass, then sit back and enjoy.

# Tropical Teaser

This fabulously indulgent blend of mango, papaya, and lychees steeped with the flavor of zesty lemon grass is sure to smooth over even the most jagged of edges.

**MAKES 1 GLASS**

1 lemon grass stalk
¼ cup/60ml water
1 cup/50g lychees
½ mango
½ papaya
½ cup/90g white grapes

1 Gently crush the lemon grass stalk, then place in a small pan with the water. Bring to the boil, then simmer for 2 minutes. Leave to cool.

2 Meanwhile, peel the lychees and remove the black pits. Peel the mango and chop the flesh. Scoop out the seeds from the papaya, then peel and chop the flesh. Press the fruit through a juicer. Strain the lemon grass water into the juice and stir.

# Red-hot Strawberry Juice

**Sip this sweet, peppery mix and feel sensations of goodwill flow through your whole body. Fiery chilies stimulate the brain to release endorphins, which naturally lift the spirits, while the strawberries and oranges offer the anti-stress nutrient, vitamin C.**

**MAKES 1 SMALL GLASS**

2 blood oranges
1 red bird's eye chili, seeded
  and finely chopped, plus
  1 chili to decorate
Scant ½ cup/60g strawberries,
  hulled

1 Squeeze the juice from the oranges and pour into a blender. Add the chopped chili and strawberries, and blend for about 45 seconds.

2 Pour into a small glass , decorate with an extra chili, and sip slowly.

# Lettuce & Juniper Lifeline

**Crisp lettuce and juniper berries give this refreshing juice a slightly bitter tang and have calming properties that will ease you into the comfort zone in no time.**

**MAKES 1 TALL GLASS**

½ tsp juniper berries
⅓ cup/80ml boiling water
8oz/225g iceberg lettuce
1½ pears
¾ cup/135g blackcurrants

1 Lightly crush the juniper berries. Place them in a small pan, pour over the boiling water and simmer for 5 minutes. Leave to cool, then strain the juice into a pitcher and discard the juniper berries.

2 Roughly chop the lettuce and pears. Press the blackcurrants through a juicer followed by the lettuce and pear. Stir in the juniper juice, pour into a glass and serve immediately.

Red-hot Strawberry Juice

Figgy Plum Smoothie

# Figgy Plum Smoothie

Rosemary gives this divine smoothie, marbled with thick and creamy yogurt, a wonderfully warm, scented flavor. The herb is also a traditional remedy for depression, so whether it's the irresistible combination of flavors and textures or the mood-enhancing properties of the ingredients, this decadent treat is sure to cheer you up and make you feel special.

**MAKES 1 TALL GLASS**

1 rosemary sprig
½ cup/120ml water
3 figs
2 plums
1 tsp lemon juice
¾ cup/180ml strained plain
  yogurt
Clear honey, to drizzle

1 Strip the leaves from the rosemary sprig and place them in a mortar. Lightly bruise the leaves with a pestle, then tip the leaves into a small pan. Add the water, bring to the boil, and then simmer very gently for 3 minutes. Remove the pan from the heat and leave to steep for about 5 minutes. Strain the liquid into a bowl and leave to cool.

2 Meanwhile, halve the figs and scoop the flesh into a blender. Cut around the crease of the plums and twist to pull apart. Lever out the pit using the tip of the knife, then roughly chop the flesh and add to the blender. Add the cooled rosemary water and blend until smooth. Stir in the lemon juice to taste.

3 Spoon a dollop of yogurt into a tall glass, and then pour over a little of the smoothie, add another dollop of yogurt, and then pour over more smoothie. Continue in this way to create a marbled effect. Finish with a dollop of yogurt, and then drizzle over a little honey and serve.

# Pink Passion

Sweet, tangy, fruity, and utterly divine, this chilled delight can't help but make you feel pampered. It's also packed with the anti-stress nutrient, vitamin C. If you prefer a smooth juice, simply strain the passion fruit pulp then stir into the juice.

**MAKES 1 GLASS**

3 oranges
½ cup/80g raspberries
1 passion fruit
Crushed ice, to serve

**1** Remove the peel from the oranges and cut into rough chunks. Press the raspberries through a juicer followed by the oranges.

**2** Cut the passion fruit in half and scoop the pulp into the juice. Stir to combine, and then pour the juice into a tall glass filled with crushed ice.

# Borage Buck-up

Borage is a traditional remedy for depression so this sweet, sticky smoothie is just the thing when you need a little comfort in your life.

**MAKES 1 GLASS**

¼ pomegranate
½ apple
½ cup/90g red grapes
1 persimmon
¼–½ lime
Borage sprig

**1** Scoop the pomegranate seeds into a sieve placed over a blender pitcher. Using the back of a spoon, press out the juice from the pomegranate seeds.

**2** Chop the apple, and then press through a juicer with the grapes. Pour into the blender.

**3** Cut the persimmon into wedges and remove the seeds and skin. Place the fruit in the blender. Blend until smooth and creamy. Stir in lime juice to taste, then pour into a glass. Add the borage and serve.

Pink Passion

Peach & Cherry Pleasure

# Peach & Cherry Pleasure

**This rich, speckled smoothie is a little taste of heaven. Peaches are rich in vitamin C, which is thought to help reduce levels of stress hormones in the blood.**

MAKES 1 GLASS

2 peaches
⅓ cup/60g cherries
½ cup/90g red grapes

1 Put the peaches in a bowl, pour over boiling water to cover and leave for 30 seconds. Drain and peel. Cut around the crease of each peach, twist the two sides apart and lever out the pit. Chop the flesh.

2 Remove the cherry pits using a cherry-pitter, then put the cherries and peaches in a blender. Push the grapes through a juicer, and then pour the juice into the blender and blend for 30 seconds until smooth. Pour into a glass and serve.

# Nectarine Thickie

**Oatmeal is a traditional calming mood-enhancer and makes a creamy base for this delicious smoothie. Unrefined brown sugar is kinder to the body than refined sugar.**

MAKES 1 TALL GLASS

1 tbsp rolled oats
3 tbsp boiling water
2 nectarines
¼ cup/40g raspberries
¼ cup/60ml milk
2 tsp soft light brown sugar
Juice ¼ lemon

1 Place the oats in a bowl, pour over the water and leave to soak for 10 minutes. Meanwhile, cut around the crease of the nectarines, twist the two sides apart and lever out the pits. Chop the flesh.

2 Put the fruit, milk and brown sugar in a blender, then add the soaked oats and blend until smooth and creamy. Stir in lemon juice to taste, pour into a glass and serve.

# Chocolate-ginger Swirl

When you need a little pampering, this rich, filling drink is just the thing—it offers you all of the pleasure and none of the guilt. Tofu and dark chocolate are both known for lifting the spirits, and ginger is often used as a traditional remedy for depression. Be sure to use silken tofu to get a superbly creamy, silky-smooth texture.

**MAKES 1 LARGE GLASS**

6 dates, chopped
½ cup/120ml boiling water
1 piece stem ginger in syrup, chopped
1oz/25g bittersweet chocolate
7oz/200g silken tofu
1 tbsp soya milk
Chocolate shavings, to decorate (optional)

1 Place the dates in a bowl, pour over the boiling water and leave to soak for 30 minutes.

2 Place the dates and soaking liquid in a blender, add the ginger and process for about 1 minute until the mixture is smooth.

3 Put the chocolate in a bowl over a pan of simmering water and heat until melted. Remove the bowl from the pan and very slowly pour in the date mixture, stirring continuously until thoroughly mixed. Chill for about 10 minutes.

4 Meanwhile, rinse out the blender, then add half the tofu and the soya milk. Blend for about 1 minute, or until smooth and frothy. Tip the mixture into a pitcher and rinse out the blender.

5 Pour the chocolate mixture into the blender, add the remaining tofu and blend until combined.

6 Spoon alternate layers of the chocolate and ginger mixtures into a tall glass, decorate with chocolate curls, if you like, and serve.

Chocolate-ginger Swirl

Icy Indulgence

# Icy Indulgence

Slushy forest fruits blended with sweet, nutty almond milk make the ultimate indulgence. Almond milk is rich in mood-enhancing B vitamins.

**MAKES 1 LARGE GLASS**

1 cup frozen soft fruits, such
   as blackberries, blueberries,
   cherries and blackcurrants,
   plus extra to decorate
1 cup almond milk

**1** Leave the frozen fruit at room temperature for about 5 minutes to thaw slightly, then tip into a blender with the almond milk.

**2** Blend until smooth and slushy, and then pour into a glass. Decorate with a spoonful of frozen fruits and serve immediately.

# Dreamy Blueberry Ripple

Enjoy the creamy, zesty swirls of the berry purée and honeyed yogurt. The blueberries will put a twinkle in your eye, while the yogurt will improve your mood.

**MAKES 1 TALL GLASS**

⅔ cup/160ml live plain yogurt
3 tbsp milk
1 tsp clear honey, plus extra
   for drizzling
½ cup/90g red grapes
½ cup/80g blueberries
1½ tsp lime juice

**1** Beat together the yogurt, milk, and honey, then set aside. Push the grapes through a juicer and pour the juicer into a blender. Reserve two or three blueberries, then add the rest to the blender. Blend to make a smooth purée. Add lime juice to taste.

**2** Spoon alternating layers of the yogurt and blueberry mixtures into a tall glass to give a rippled effect, finishing with a spoonful of the yogurt mixture. Drizzle over a little more honey and decorate with the reserved blueberries.

# Weights and measures

The following conversions and equivalents will provide useful guidelines for international readers to follow. There's just one golden rule to remember when you're preparing your ingredients: always stay with one system of measurement—that way you'll achieve the best results from these recipes.

## Liquid ingredients

| | | |
|---|---|---|
| ½ tsp | = | 2.5ml |
| 1 tsp | = | 5ml |
| 1 tbsp. | = | 15ml |
| 2 tbsp | = | 30ml |
| 3 tbsp | = | 45ml |
| ¼ cup | = | 60ml |
| ⅓ cup | = | 80ml |
| ½ cup | = | 125ml |
| ⅔ cup | = | 160ml |
| ¾ cup | = | 180ml |
| 1 cup | = | 250ml |
| 1½ cups | = | 375ml |
| 2 cups | = | 500ml |
| 3 cups | = | 750ml |
| 4 cups | = | 1 liter |
| 5 cups | = | 1.2 liters |
| 6 cups | = | 1.5 liters |
| 8 cups | = | 2 liters |

## Dry ingredients

| | | |
|---|---|---|
| ¼oz | = | 10g |
| ½oz | = | 15g |
| ¾oz | = | 20g |
| 1oz | = | 25g |
| 1½oz | = | 40g |
| 2oz | = | 50g |
| 2½oz | = | 65g |
| 3oz | = | 75g |
| 3½oz | = | 90g |
| 4oz | = | 115g |
| 4½oz | = | 130g |
| 5oz | = | 150g |
| 5½oz | = | 165g |
| 6oz | = | 175g |
| 6½oz | = | 185g |
| 7oz | = | 200g |
| 7½oz | = | 215g |
| 8oz | = | 225g |

| | | |
|---|---|---|
| 9oz | = | 250g |
| 10oz | = | 275g |
| 11oz | = | 300g |
| 12oz | = | 350g |
| 14oz | = | 400g |
| 15oz | = | 425g |
| 1lb | = | 450g |
| 1¼lb | = | 500g |
| 1½lb | = | 675g |
| 2lb | = | 900g |
| 2¼lb | = | 1kg |
| 3–3½lb | = | 1.5kg |
| 4–4½lb | = | 1.75kg |
| 5–5¼lb | = | 2.25kg |
| 6lb | = | 2.75kg |

## Measurements

| | | |
|---|---|---|
| ¼in | = | 5mm |
| ½in | = | 1cm |
| ¾in | = | 2cm |
| 1in | = | 2.5cm |
| 1½in | = | 4cm |
| 2in | = | 5cm |
| 2½in | = | 6.5cm |
| 3in | = | 7.5cm |
| 4in | = | 10cm |
| 5in | = | 12.5cm |

# Glossary

The following glossary of culinary terms will provide useful guidelines for international readers to follow.

**arugula:** rocket
**baby tomatoes:** cherry tomatoes
**beet:** beetroot
**bok choy:** pak choi
**ogen melon:** galia melon
**pitcher:** jug
**plain yogurt:** natural yogurt
**red bell pepper:** red pepper
**rockmelon:** cantaloupe melon
**strained plain yogurt:** Greek yogurt
**yellow bell pepper:** yellow pepper

# Index